strata

strata
ewa chrusciel

OMNIDAWN PUBLISHING
RICHMOND, CALIFORNIA
2018

Cover painting by Julie Püttgen: *Cloudmapping: Becalmed*, 2008.
Watercolor and gouache on paper, 16"x12"
www.108namesofnow.com & www.unlessanduntil.info.

Cover typeface: Kabel LT Std
Interior typeface: Garamond 3 LT Std

Cover & interior design by Cassandra Smith

Offset printed in the United States
by Edwards Brothers Malloy, Ann Arbor, Michigan
On 55# Enviro Natural 100% Recycled 100% PCW
Acid Free Archival Quality FSC Certified Paper

Strata is the winner of the 2009 Emergency Press International Book Contest
and was first published by Emergency Press in 2011

Library of Congress Cataloging-in-Publication Data

Names: Chrusciel, Ewa, author.
Title: Strata / Ewa Chrusciel.
Description: Oakland, California : Omnidawn Publishing, 2018. | Includes
    bibliographical references.
Identifiers: LCCN 2017052619 | ISBN 9781632430564 (pbk. : alk. paper)
Classification: LCC PS3603.H78 A6 2018 | DDC 811/.6--dc23
LC record available at https://lccn.loc.gov/2017052619

Published by Omnidawn Publishing, Oakland, California
www.omnidawn.com (510) 237-5472 (800) 792-4957
10 9 8 7 6 5 4 3 2 1
ISBN: 978-1-63243-056-4

ACKNOWLEDGMENTS

Grateful acknowledgment is made to the *Boston Review* which published the first six poems as well as to the editors of the following publications, in whose pages some of these poems first appeared, or are forthcoming:

Aufgabe Magazine

Colorado Review

Poetry Wales

Lana Turner One

Process

hot metal bridge

Sawbuck

Mandorla

Entelechy

XCP: Cross Cultural Poetics:

American Letters and Commentary

Canary 8

Squaw Valley Review (2009)

Taiga (2009)

ERA I

ERA II

ERA III

ERA IV

CODA

But, among us there is a hoopoe who dictates
his letters to the olive tree of exile.

Mahmoud Darwish, "The Hoopoe"

We select, we construct, we compose our pasts and hence make
fictional characters of ourselves as it seems we must to remain
sane.

William H. Gass, "Fiction and the Figures of Life"

ERA I

na   *no*   *la*

They come as yellow secrets. They bilocate. They are ubiquitous as Tartar
cheeks. They air the air. We bury them. They hover as hummingbirds,
calculating their rates of return. They come in volcanic lavish. They come
in lekking crowds. They come as juncos. They perch on branches like
monk hedgehogs. The come as seven foxes jumping to meet innocence.
They tingle. Sorrelic apparitions. They speck in the morning. They
thistle. There is a tigress mother wanting to trim your hair. They come
in high-strung beads and scatter into our vessels. They dot. They come as
hard-faced dybbuks. They are relics of grief and light. They re-colonize.
They want to rent one line. They rap on our door with churned-up
grains, tides, whispers. They come as drafts of juniper. They spread on
the floor as a cross. We bury them. They come in black chadors. Rising
and swaying parasols. Thin as grass. They come as silver jaguars. They
want to break down. They come to insulate us with snow. Do you hear
them? They try to get where they belong. With forget-me-nots. They
have fancy hats. They pebble across the floor. They fall from marigold
trees and lie crucified on the road. Get up and sing. We are burying them
in staccato rhythm. Others—miniscule kisses. Some as heavy footsteps.
We are burying them. They rise and accrete. They trespass. They beat
electric letters in the air. They come to us. They come with swinging hips.
They come as minnows. They come in wrinkles. They come as a host of
molecules. They swarm into this lighthouse. They pinch like too much
love. They hop always to a higher branch. They come invincible. They
come to torture. They come to soothe. They come for romance. They flip
and tremble tiny farewells. They come as mustard seeds. Do you see them
in a mulberry tree? They slide down the needles. They come as growth on
wolf trees, the dead winking. They air the air. They come to forgive. They
ask for forgiveness. They come as hyphae. They come as hostages. They
come as clogged streets. They come in slow trains. Burning bushes, doves,
manna, the blood of horses' necks. They come as purgatory souls. They
chip off the wall. In loops and whorls. They come in giggles. They come
in almonds. They come to eye us, inside our panther skins.

what's the evidence of belonging

Kraina na bosaka. Your first sentence will always be in your native lung.
Grandma had a big drawer with sweets she distributed freely. She farted.
She chased us with loaves of bread soaked in honey. Love is thick and
yellow. I would bite her or pinch on her buttocks. Love is pinching.
Grandpa was an owl. He saw the Holy Mother in the fields. *Encounter
is a linguistic cousin of country.* I prayed every night she would not appear to
me. My nose was too broad for his taste, so he told me to keep it squeezed
with my fingers for 15 minutes a day. When he died, I refused to go in
for fear he would criticize me—still. My neighbor died in the window
from lightning. Lightning is a strange apparition. A big moment yellow.
In storms I close the windows. My brother liked to throw the cats into
the well. For his birthday, he would bring my uncle nettles. Then there
was Tigress Mother. She would pretend to be dying when I did not want
to eat ham. She brought the precious stones home. When the moon was
full, she took me to a neighbor to trim my hair. I was her biggest cat.
Our father stuffed us with apples. I ate so many I became the apple of his
eye. He caught mice for me so I could run with them on a leash like a
queen of the courtyard. When there were no mice, I would be overcome
by strange despairs. In the face of no ailment, my father asked me to spit
and catch. Instead, I would let the budgies free. To be attached to trinkets,
extravagant frills and flounces.

I lose home every time I send it

We mourn places as well as people. *We would like only for once to get where we are already.* I count these sentences in Polish. Lexicons trespass; cross-code breakdowns. It is strange to see myself from where I was. I've grown. I feed the birds. You asked what is the size of my radiance? I cultivate it. Until cross turns into wings. The peacock of the Sun wakes me up with the reflexes of light. Sometimes the light will pebble across the floor and tickle my eyes. Places are extensions of people. What illness springs from the lost place? *Horror Vacui.* Your first sentence will always be in your native lung. *Encounter is a linguistic cousin of country.* To know where I am is to know that I am determinately there. Bodily here in relation to an already known there or set of theres. Yet there are layers of invisible belonging. I eat a lot of ginger and play with emerald children. What are the true desires in this disguise? I fantasize having a mynah bird. Instead, I would let the budgies free. When there were no mice, I would be overcome by strange despairs. It got even worse when there was no snow. The monotony of it all would kill even a seahorse. In the face of no ailment, my father would ask me to spit and catch. A big moment yellow. I cannot go on. I have other ontological commitments.

is there something down
         by the water
                  keeping itself from us

We are woven of minuscule desires. They swirl in myriad wakes like
minnows. If you think how many niches, crevices, and rocks they could
inhabit. On Valentine's Day, you borrowed a tulip from somebody else. I
ate it. I only pretended to be crazy. Now I pretend to be normal. Or it's
always rather a decision. You said not even grass has such thin hair. After
that kissing was much more fiery. Can our lives still cross through the
remote thinking? I am just on the other side of the mirror. *Horror vacui.*
Everything preserved under a glass wall. What illness springs from the
lost place? Places are extensions of people. I count everything in Polish.
In a certain sense I did commit suicide in order to live. I prefer reason. It's
a sacrifice of the immediate. Swinging causes too much seasickness. You
cannot take it all. Offer. Sacrifice does not kill, but preserve, make it holy.
Until wings turn into a cross. However noble, if we do things on our own,
we are the enemies of grace. Odysseus was noble. Nevertheless Dante put
him in hell, precisely for that reason. Hell is based on justice. Heaven is
grace. Nobody deserves it.

always drown in good company

I have been secretly storing snow in my apartment so I can ski from one room to another. *Kraina na bosaka.* If a pinch of salt is burned, it gives off light. What about suffering? I break in order to reveal. Repetition is an accretion. If we think persistently of somebody, won't they think of us? Maybe thoughts live in their own worlds? They too travel outside. They pack and unpack. 13 has control over me. It is an unfinished project. Can our lives still cross through remote thinking? Turn wings until a cross. Instead I write. Omnivorous cosmopolitan pages of white. I wish they would take off like cranes, beating electric letters in the air. *Encounter is a linguistic cousin of country.* I eat a lot of ginger and play with emerald children. I exercise too much. Paper cuts deep my skin. I forget and grab it child-like, curious about its smell and usage. The first swimming lessons. My father, inspired by new Russian discoveries, would drop me right into water. Maybe it was too late: I was four or three. He would pull me out when I was already drowning. Russians invent, fathers adapt. Mother would get into such despairs she wanted to drown herself. With us. However noble, if we do things only on our own, we are the enemies of grace.

if light is both particle and wave
is light schizophrenic

The lamps are the whales of light. How many orphaned words swarm into
this lighthouse. They swirl in myriad wakes like minnows. Think what
fancy hats they have now. With forget-me-nots. If you think how many
niches, crevices, and rocks they could inhabit. Encounter means we are
made to begin always. Why do I start with an old sentence? Repetition
is innovation. Repetition is an. Crowded loneliness. Sometimes the
light will pebble across the floor and tickle my eyes. Dante would put
Normal, Illinois somewhere in Purgatory in his abridged version. Those
who enjoy life too much end up here. Or those who believe in speech acts
and think the name will save them from life's aberrations. I wish chairs
would grow wings. Only trees can really scrape the skies. You have the
tattoo of light on your face. Your wrinkles glitter into spider webs. This
is the circumference of my radiance. *We would like only for once to get where
we are already.* In storms I close the windows. Swinging causes too much
seasickness. Nobody deserves it. The light tickles me. The whale giggles
a cascade. 27 is not merely enough. It's always rather a decision. She is
a confused sunflower. I counted again in Polish. Wild(d)éornes—Old
English place of wild deer. The squirrels lie crucified on the road.

time hanged itself

                                            on a tree branch

Perhaps the day Sequoia met Christ, they started to sprout. They became
self-reflexive giants. Father was in Solidarity. Mother was so afraid she
would hide the underground papers in the rabbits' cage. During Russian,
I would stand up and say: "Lvov was ours." The teacher called my parents
twice. My father called me a little patriot. Now I am in a foreign land.
Am I displaced voluntarily? Bodily "here" in relation to an already
known "there" or set of "theres." I live inside a dictionary. Lexicons re-
territorialize, trespass. I eat a lot of ginger and fantasize about having
a mynah bird. *Kraina na bosaka.* In the summer the walls were buzzing
entities. They were Jacob's ladders for flies. Our grandma used to say that
garbage men would come and take us. Whenever we heard a garbage
van, we crawled under the table. Love is pinching. I practiced writing
by rewriting the newspapers. Alpacas are fluffy and meek. Whenever my
parents were leaving, I banged my head against the well. Well was my
wailing wall. Mountains in snowy yarmulkes are the reversed cathedrals.
Snowflakes are tiny dots of waltzing light. As a child I was fascinated with
drunks. I would stop and engage them in conversation. How fascinating
to see the loops and whorls of their words. That they might take off like
cranes, beating electric letters in the air. Instead, I let the budgies free.
Country precedes encounter. A man has grown his roots into a woman.
We would like only for once to get where we are already. Your last sentence will
always be in your native lung.

today light in itself
capable to paint

Encounter. Luminous brown calmness. You said you've been always
fascinated by the symmetry of. Half given; the other half hidden. Do
you see a mulberry in a mustard seed? Which part—insanity? X-rays of
hands through layered rings. Anything carved into them heals into black
scars, recording the event. Undying iterations of this moment. Flicker
of memories. My mother would sit by me and point to his supposed
mistresses. Her theories—elaborate. She collected the evidence. Once
she asked me to check his toiletries bag. I was little. There was a rubber.
I flushed it in the toilet. Or it's always, rather, a decision. I eat a lot of
ginger and play with emerald children. Everything preserved under the
glass wall. When you pass by with her, you say it's cold. Anyway, there are
too many divorces. I would let the budgies free. What are the true desires
in this disguise? I forget it and grab it, curious about its smell and usage.
My dad is a bee-master. Love is thick and yellow. Bees, like Pythias, offer
him solemn bows. Perhaps all illnesses spring from absence of love. The
void must be filled somehow. If only we were decentralized. *If you could
only grasp that you are not the center of things. The center is He, and He, too, finds
no love—*

sometimes sinking
in imitative thoughtlessness

The threat of *atopia* calls forth a veritable *ontomania*—an irrational desire
to have and to know as much determinate presence as possible. Fear of
having an empty mind is really the same fear. Should I call him? Instead
I write. The lamps are the whales of light. Instead I let the budgies
free. We found a wriggling egg in our garden. We warmed it up by the
bonfire until it broke open. Baby Quail. We had to feed it with milk.
Even mother warmed up. We took it to our grandparents. They told me
it died when it tried to fly. I suspect someone accidentally squeezed it
with a cooking pan. I am just on the other side of the mirror. Everything
preserved under the glass wall. We do not know how to remain in repose.
Is that why the Tibetans tie their children to the poles—in case they
might wander off. I was called a chocolate missie. My parents would hide
the chocolate in the highest cabinets. I would pile desks and chairs and
climb. Once I fell, and lying on the floor, could not catch my breath.
We would like only for once to get where we are already. And all of it for the
love of. My grandma had a big drawer with sweets she distributed freely.
What are the true desires in this disguise? During fights my father would
remind my mother she was a Tartar. You said not even grass has such thin
hair. Everything was under the custody of 13. It entered us, perplexed, by
the theory of our non-incidence. The signs were sprouting. Too discernible
in their silence.

does dwelling   *occur*   *in the box*

A man is insofar as he dwells. I've been busy watching aspens. They depend on a disturbance—mainly fire—for regeneration. Yet they display wounds very clearly. Anything carved into them heals into black scars, recording the event. The clothes I liked the most would disappear. I had to lock my wardrobe. Anything I liked too much was under suspicion. When she discovered my wardrobe was closed, she thought there were drugs inside. I was her biggest cat. In a basket case. In storms I close the windows. Dwelling—Old English *dwalde*—go astray, err, wander. Lord God! Ivory-billed woodpecker is back. The land that runs barefoot. Rather we always go through spaces such that we experience them as near and remote. What if this place is not a matter of arbitrary placing? *Horror vacui*. The fear of empty mind is really the same fear. Does God have the address? Is it also a box that God has? My dad bought himself a mountain. A hill, rather, but whenever I speak of him, my imagination turns. He produces honey there. He's a bee-master. For bees he is a very cosmonaut with his out-of-the-blue accordion. Or he is a minister and his pipe is an incense. Bees, like Pythias, offer him bows. On Valentine's you borrowed a tulip. Did it have thirteen petals? Signs were discernible in their silence. Until they disassembled. Did we unscrew mystery?

I see colonies of ants   *marching in*
funeral

Mandibles make me think of ants, almonds. The size of my radiance is volcanic lavish. Or giggling neurosis. That's how cross turns into chairs. Flapping, flapping on its flimsy wings. Wood coming alive and on fins soaring. I thought I was doing anything I wanted with memory. Instead memory is doing anything she wants with me. Should I really count the sentences? I prefer reason. *If we go down into ourselves we find that we possess exactly what.* I was called a chocolate missy. My parents would hide chocolate in the highest cabinets. Once I fell and could not catch my breath. I wish chairs would grow wings. Perhaps this is a hell. This relying on the sense of adventure. And *imping*. However noble, if we do things only on our own, we are the enemies of grace. Odysseus was noble. Nevertheless Dante put him in hell, precisely for that reason. Country is a linguistic cousin of encounter. Hebrew word *Makom* means both God and Place. Do you see a seed in a mulberry tree? Then does God have the address? Today the ants moved in—subleasing for the summer. Will they pass my feet?

water   *has*   *memory*

Kiedy wróciłaś się do mieszkania i usiadłaś na podłodze z bezsilnością
dziecka mówiąc, że nie możesz znaleźć portfela. Broken Porcelain. And
how you left and came back and crouching on the floor could not find
your wallet. As if the house was on fire and all your savings and treasures
(and us) were somehow there. In the hidden corridors of your purse.
Zbudowana z drobinek światła i kolorów. Pochylona nad swoją ulotnością.
Zmartwiona, że możesz się rozsypać jak koraliki. You wanted so much.
More than Reality could Give. So you Sold yourself to the Underworld.
Sneaking Out Delicacies That Were Poisonous. Those Neatly Woven
Threads of Dowry Started to Seep Through Your Hands. Seeping through.
Poseuse de Dos. De Face. De Profile. Built from Atoms of Light and Colors.
Beads dispaired. Your Nerves. Scattered into the map of our suffering.
The cavities of your wallet well with water. There is a spring there now.
High-strung beads. That dispersed. I'm trying to collect. It's like picking
up each penny. Which might have saved the world. The first swimming
lessons. Seeping in through the dark cavities of your wallet.

mene

   mene

 tekel   **upharsin**

You ride numbers like the Delphic Charioteer. High-strung
beads. His horses the ink will fossilize like them like him.
Numb will your arm be. Entangled in your hair. Entangled
in the pupils of your eyes. Entangled in the circuit
of your mouth. Numb will your arm be. You taste their
detail, the weariness of white. You accompany the *sfumato*
of an existence.

        Time   will   hear   the

    flutter   of   your   numbers

        patiently   chanted   numerous   litany   mantra

        mandalayour   faithful Brahmanism   one   day   you

        receive   the   seven   ciphers of seven

        we   would   like   only for once

    to   get   where   we   are   you   check

        the pulse   of   space   time's heartbeat in

    undying   effacement   facing

ERA II

topology   must   triumph

over   no   place

I multiply my flats blueprints palimpsests. This is a reproduction of
Being. Friends, I'm writing to you from the U.S., where reality shows and
Viagra get shipped to you overnight though you did not ask for them. You
get all the prospects of singles in the neighborhood in your daily bottle
of milk patiently browsing outside. I'm trying to be socially involved: I
watch Average Joe, War on Terrorism, *Empire Strikes Back.* I also date on
a full scale. Our secret meetings Between the Rockies and Appalachians.
He is unpredictable. Whenever he comes near I tremble and lie down.
We define ourselves on Fujita Scale. When it's up I toss and hurl. Yet I
learn that his size is not necessarily indication of his intensity. Any time
I deliberately put myself above ground I am putting myself in his arms.
My Tornado Alley. The tip of the day is: when you come round, stay close
to the ground. Stay close to the ground. The threat of *atopia* calls forth
a veritable ontomania, irrational desire to have and to know as much
determinate presence as possible. Fear of having an empty mind is really
the same fear. If Hebrew *Makom* means both God and Place, does God
have the address? Encounter is a linguistic cousin of country. A man is
insofar as he dwells. I suffer from excess. *A fish in water that suffers of thirst.*
The desire to be everybody. A desire to have everything. To transgress.
The size of my radiance is precisely that of volcanic lavish. *A sponge
suffering, because it cannot saturate itself. A river, suffering because the reflections
of clouds and trees are not clouds and trees.*

Corpus   Christi

Kanonicza Street. In the windows Holy Marys basking, like dignified
flower-pots. On the sheets of rain the divine and human features brailing.
The procession of cobbles. Raising and swaying parasols. Coming to
Grodzka Street. Gilded lions, brass angels, (elephant anorexic) stirred
in worship. Proceeding petals by petals. Streets clogging and kneeling.
All the gilded dust chipping off Market Square. Sealing up in yodels—
merging with the Invisible Body. Is this the world you died for? Leaving
lashings of froufrou cloaks. Flirting Violins. Waltzing glass wines.
Elations of masques. So lean the wings of angels. Nesting the eyes high
above. We put you high up. They will always look for you in the vertically
climbing abstractions. Where they have elevated you to cast you down (for
you are the Holy one, for you are Aloof and Ungraspable). You are in my
father's wrinkles. In the slow decay of his body. I saw you sitting on those
benches among the Beslan children. You were breaking the bread whose
little tiny vessels started firing. Your extended palm; nerves exploded and
scattered into the map of our suffering. I'm trying to collect. High-strung
beads. Which might have saved the world. Which dispersed.

death most reveals　　　　　　　　　*itself by single shoes*

Scattered on the street. All the tracks covered. Only the sole still lurks.
And there, gaping pits. A shoelace still shivers. As a child I would sit
in the room and crave some accident. To be an onlooker. A *voyeur*. In
the face of no ailment, my father would ask me to spit and catch. Here
shoes are hung on electric wires. My American students tell me it used
to be a sign that somebody died. Or a secret sign for drug dealers. When
we were little, we would drive with our parents to a beach in Bulgaria.
People would stop us and ask for lipsticks, chewing-gums, medicines.
There is no life without a reimbursement. Once when we were crossing
the border, my father woke me up. There was a dead body on the road.
Big moment yellow. I am just on the other side of the mirror. Everything
preserved under the glass wall. Every summer when I go to visit Poland,
the shoes are there on the road. A veritable ontomania, a reproduction of
being. Non-bodily here in relation to an already known there or set of
there, where, here. *There is no there, there.* Things break in order to reveal. A
shoe would like to burst forth. When my grandma died, I refused to take
a photograph with her. Only after the funeral, at the cemetery, my face
resurrected. I saw her in a white wedding dress with my grandfather. Next
day she woke me up at four in the morning and I wrote my first poem.

wild   *(d)*   *éornes*

In Bob Moon, this drunk, black as soot, God lives. In him, evil and good spirits commune. The first time Kasia and I went to Colorado, Bob—a property manager—took care of us. I was doing sociolinguistic research and I secretly recorded Bob. *I kill'em—mountain lions, poke their eyes out, poke'm out, cut their throat, kill'em or they gonna kill you. You got to be straight. You hit directly in the eyes, you poke'm out. You think I'm joking? They ain't too friendly—Ha, ha, ha I don't take shit from nobody.* It's those people's fault. You tell'em. I'm a redneck. I'm a cowboy. I don't take shit from nobody. Bob's style displays high levels of informality and casualness. It is affectedly charged; high pitched voice, sharp contours and exclamation marks help to convey his temper. *I ain't no joking. Patty Ann Stuart. Sweetest, nicest, most innocent girl. I ruined her.* His highly emphatic style, the use of gestures and characteristic laughter introducing almost every third sentence, makes Bob's speech animated and informal. *I did! Ruined her! Heh, heh!* Salient features include use of double negative, characteristic of working-class speech. The speed of his speech is rapid and he constantly swallows or abbreviates certain consonants, such as in: "kill'em," (line 5); "poke'm" (line 7); "tell'em" (line 11). On my birthday I hoped that deer would be in the graven horned road continually rising before us. Instead someone was following us in a truck. On a dusty and empty road. We pulled over. It was Bob. Almost bashfully he asked: You want me take you to the place with deer?

all   *the*   *narratives*

exploded

You say there are no angels yet you see a host of molecules descend and
congregate. 330 children in loops and whorls. Now, in Beslan children
know how to play hide and seek in school. Particled skin, feet, fingers.
Hair and nails growing. Laughing kookaburras fly. You see a host
of molecules. Stellar dendrites {crystal partition space} descend and
congregate. 1,200 hostages in loops and whorls *with intersecting arrays*.
You say there are no arrays of parallel lives. Those kids enter us hard-
faced, like dybbuks. The Host beyond crisps. 176 orphans. Hair and
nails growing. Those kids enter us hard-faced like dybbuks straight into
the belly of a frozen whale. We'll have to raise them. 1,200 hostages in
loops and whorls. There is gravity and grace and these lines interwoven
together. Miniscule plots which exploded hair and nails growing straight
into the belly of a frozen whale. We'll have to raise them. There is gravity
and grace—these lines woven together. Pebbling into your eyelids, bags,
pockets, there is gravity and grace fully furnishing the hard-faced space.
Through the specked air archangel surged. Coiling into the tattoos of
mourning light. Your eyelid flutters cascades. And now undying iterations
of this moment. Between you and you—a grave child. Between you and
me, the cross—and two meeting lines for the few seconds produce motion.
Amid the fixity of lines loving gaze. Insnailed into the coils of your name.
You say No Angels. We'll have to raise them.

the roads diverged in a wood

and I took all of them

Can all those histories jump out at you simultaneously? From the front, back, top, bottom, and sides? Explosion that occurs simultaneously everywhere. I suffer from excess. I multiply my blueprints, palimpsests, flats. This is a being of reproduction. To know where I am is to know that I am determinately there. Bodily here in relation to an already known there or set of theres. There is no there. Yet there are layers of invisible belonging. To have all. To transgress. Writing will not do, to fill in the billions years of loneliness. A veritable ontomania. Irrational desire to have and to know as much determinate presence as possible. Unborn designs circle over unpatched roofs. Multiple polarities of a text—in which relativity means the infinite variability of experience as well as the infinite multiplication of possible ways of measuring things—won't do in the face of billions of years of solitude. Of cooling of the universe. Amidst disruptive forces of indeterminacy and discontinuity, there is still an organizing rule which governs all the relations. Even God needs companionship. Lexicons reterritorialize, trespass. A crowded loneliness. What if this place is not a matter of arbitrary placing? There are places. Pattern masquerades as randomness. The universe has every possible history. Some of these histories will contain people like us. They never stay together—they know that nothing stays. Thus does mystery never stay. I never possessed you. You are always and never now and there. I just imagined holding you for a moment; but, really, can you hold water? Instead, I let the budgies free. After feeding the birds take off—beat the electric letters in the air.

snow   a   martyr

To be in love is like going out to check your mailbox. Do not get me
wrong. If you love him how prove he loves you too. We began by
evanescence. A remote chance that you meet in the mailbox. Do you see a
mulberry tree in a mustard seed? The mailbox does not keep the record.
I was afraid of my grandfather. He exuded coldness. And yet you were
a spitting image of him. And I loved you more than any dictionaries. I
studied hoopoes to contain you. You said not even grass has such thin hair.
In time of suffering, I insulate myself with snow. For a moment white
albatrosses fall from the sky and become their own species of nouns; pray
why chase each stalk of wounded light? The beauty possessed wounds
and dwindles. White anarchy of their feathers. In a moment, the Snow
Destruction Company will come to level this paralyzing powder and
carry it away to the gas chambers, slaughterhouses, camps. It is a sin
against Holy Albatrosses—this ingratitude. We suffer from excess. There
is a nobility in asking the same thing over and over again. Each broken
snowflake becomes a broken coastline. The line of infinite affection—
squeezed into limited space. Engraved on the palm of your hand. Whose
nerves explode and scatter into the map of our suffering.
The hour we knew nothing of each other.

even God needs companionship

We were eating fish soup. I said sin is a waste of time. It is settling for less. *Sin and art have something in common*—you said. *They both promise happiness. Sin betrays the promise in pain and destruction while art merely defers the happiness and makes the promise again, generating an endless pleasant string of promises that are not so much broken as endlessly deferred. It's like the end of Dante's* Paradiso *when he's gone so far that the only thing left to see is God himself but Dante leaves the pilgrim craning over an abyss with everything again infinitely deferred.* I said: My longing is preceded by endless waiting. I wade through tiny spinning atoms of affection. What a gift—this connectedness. I said I would quote you here. You said: *What, am I writing this whole thing now???* I said: however noble, if we do things only on our own, we are the enemies of grace. *Besides, If ideas are like air, you can't steal them.* You said: *If the being of God is mysterious, what happens to our spirit after death must be equally unspeakable. They make it sound like a freaking hog roast where the Pepsi flows eternally. Just where I wouldn't want to be for eternity.* I said: God has the address. *Ultimately, the happiness that art promises, the greatest happiness it promises, is "to see a landscape as it is when I am not there,"*—you said. I say: we need to color and tame landscape. The only thing that saves it is. Or rather, incarnation. *Man has to perform an act of incarnation, for he is disembodied. "Desincarne" by his imagination. What comes to us from Satan is our imagination.* Can landscape be incarnated? Places are extensions of people. There is no country without encounter. We begin with evanescence.

pentecost 1

You wrote: that explains a lot. This morning I woke up clapping! Luigi thought it was for him but after about half an hour of non-stop clapping even he thought it was a little weird. I thought that it meant I'd come down with Tourette's syndrome or some other mental illness that results in uncontrollable behavior. Thank goodness it was merely the Holy Spirit descending on me in great waves of applause on Whitsuntide. Miss you, C. PS I've done some preliminary drawings of our villa in rural Poland. The garden is in the shape of a Chopin Nocturne, if you can imagine that. I'm thinking we won't actually need a house. We'll be like Lear and Tom the fool (I can be the fool, it's okay) walking around on the heath saying, "Blow wind and crack your cheeks." Doesn't that sound nice? I hope that being a deranged patriarch will work for you. Actually for some reason the left hand stopped clapping suddenly last night around 10:30, which is pretty damned awkward. The right hand continues but because the left hand isn't meeting it I think I've destroyed my right elbow. At any rate, the whole forearm and hand now dangles sort of uselessly from my damaged elbow and flaps back and forth still trying to clap. I mean, this is some determined (and painful!) Holy Spirit. I wish it would back off for a day or so because this can't be good for. You said: I take you so much to heart that your soul is causing large growths on my body where your abundance of spirit exceeds my capacity. It's as if I need to imagine I'm in love with you in order to maintain a certain energy or feeling to keep me moving forward toward something that has nothing to do with you. You're more like a midwife than a mistress. I say: I am a landscape that you just managed to incarnate. Or a landscape where all orphaned chances take on unabated meaning. So it is perhaps more than just making me or you less lonely. I wade from *kairos* to *kairos*. We crave seasons, red-letter days. We wish they took off like cranes, beating electric letters in the air. *We would like only for once to get where we are already. If we go down into ourselves we find that we possess exactly what we desire.* It is not your face I desire. It is not your body. I desire. Something inside. Someplace I can't arrive.

dear owl

Thank you for stopping by Normal on 23rd March 2004 and perching
on this little pot-tree in front of "Other Ports." It's been a week and
I'm still thinking about you. Thank you for overlooking the fact that
the little porch of the other port was by no means a cannon. And those
passing by were no mice. I am delighted that taking into consideration
those slight landscape changes, you nicely dozed off, replacing a little
statute of Buddha bored to death with mercantile day-to-day meditation.
I (having a little weakness, Zelig's syndrome) perched on the little bench
opposite and like you, tried to maintain my balance. People passing by
with fully-fledged American smiles and understanding were saying, "It's
nice to be taking the air outside." Some more observant would look up
and see you and exclaim: "Oh, it can't be real." Being a responsive person
in every possible manner, I examined you critically. Thought of Dürer:
Das Käuzechen, then the other possible names: *civetta*, *choutte*, *otus asio*,
bubo virginianus, Amirus Barakus. Explosion of owl. The desire to have
all. Horror vacui. Dear Eastern Red Phase Owl. Find this poem enclosed.
Please consider this for your beakation. With every kind wind, yours
tuftully, E.C., the family of *crex paternus*, wading crane.

Dear Owl, I sent you a letter a week ago or so. No answer received. I wonder where have you been? Perhaps my letter was too informal for your highbrowness. Perhaps a bit too editorializing. You are a bird of considerable sageness. There is no country without an encounter. Please reconsider my poem. Please find corrections enclosed. Attached below: Eastern Red Phase, all day clenching with little tufty claws to one chosen branch of a little tree-pot in front of the "Other Ports" shop on the North Main street in Normal. "It can't be real" people passing by said. Each feather swaying to only one key. Can it be real? Little Eskimo. I will never write to you again until I have flown a mile in your fluffy moccasins, in your fluffy moccasins.

would fire be so gentle?

First it was a mad love of electrons. An electron sets on a journey
and another electron comes in. When they get closer the attraction is
magnetic, so one electron shakes off the photon and the other absorbs
the photon—gets a kick and lurches in another direction. They never
stay together—they know that nothing stays. The simultaneous histories
wave and cross and this wave function makes them equal. The universe
has every possible history. Some of those histories will contain people like
us, some of them will not. Which history do we live on? Which history
chooses us? Do those histories cross and join? Which plane is our love
still on? Could we ever have children? If everything moves around us
and becomes modified constantly by the speed then we never even meet
our children. They never stay. So does mystery never stay. Or, it always
remains mystery by never staying on as mystery—modified in each
capillary second. To think of a final resting place then is a contradiction
of elementary logic. *The motion of "now" occurs in a time shorter than the
blink of an eye, since a second of time delineates a segment of space spread out like
a 186,000-mile-long caterpillar. Imagine you are Alice, as you move through
this "caterpillar" at ever-increasing speed.* Space contracts. When you achieve
the speed of light, the space outside of our frame of reference merges and
becomes infinitely thin. At such speed, time and movement halt. *There
is no there, there.* I never possessed you. I just imagined holding you for
a moment, but *can you hold the water?* A man has to possess something.
I created birds out of you. But even birds stay only as long as you feed
them.

annunciation   *of*   *light*

Wherever I go you let in the light. Ripple.
Unforseen cataract, soft brush of truth. Reminder of.
Where I belong. To the reflections. Of light. On altars.
Wherever I go you let in not enough. I stopped.
Collecting Evidence. For your existence
I stopped collecting the evidence and yet there are
layers of invisible belonging

sometimes   light   will   pebble

across   the   floor   and   tickle   my   eyes   coiling

into   the   tattoos   of   mourning   light   I

stopped   collecting   pebbles   into   your   eyelids   bags

pockets   cataract   evidence   for

ERA III

each day   *a crescendo of*

absence

April 8th, 2005. Rather than funeral march, the pirouette of cardinal robes inside wind. Perhaps the day Sequoia met Christ, they started to sprout, and became self-reflexive giants. You are in the box, being sent to everybody. What a gift. This connectedness. And yet the woods live: 47,000 stems sprout from the root of a single tree. The High German word for building—*buan*—means to dwell, to remain, to stay in place. The Hebrew word *Makom* means both God and Place. God has the address. I am here without my place. I multiply my flats blueprints palimpsests (topology must triumph over no place). This is a reproduction of Being. The threat of *atopia* calls forth a veritable *ontomania*, irrational desire to have and know as much determinate presence as possible. Fear of having an empty mind is the same fear. To say that mortals are is to say that in dwelling they persist through spaces by virtue of their stay. It wasn't a funeral march but the pirouette of cardinal robes. Old English *dwalde*—to go astray, err, wander. Always waiting, we are always waiting for a message, for a momentary dwelling where our heart could place its tired messages. Leaves of winged forks from inside explode. Each of us is *Alef* and *Bet*, a home for the spirit. The *alef* the silence of Spirit from which all sound flows. The *bet* means "house." I've been busy watching aspen trees. A largest living organism. In a high wind the leaves will clump together and fight the horizontal force of the air. Outside solitary and quaking, we make underground passages.

pentecost 2

I go to Lunkers for Ana's birthday. He is a bird. I knew this story would
be continued. An electron sets out on a journey and another electron
comes in. You said you were afraid I would never call back. When they
get closer, the attraction is magnetic, so that one electron shakes off the
photon and the other absorbs the photon—gets a kick and moves in
another direction. Now we have our wasabi ginger staircase. What
an eruption of brown. Why are we so omnivorous? Sex is what we say and
not what we do. The paint will splash, dissipate. We could grow beautiful
little almonds. The snaky-twigged branches coil up. In dire worship, the
air horny, clumped up. I wade through tiny spinning atoms. Love is thick
and yellow. The entire world is an egg. Universe has every possible history
(which history will choose us to live on?) and yet one method. It—a
crying infant—needs someone to produce the loud shushing noise which
imitates what the fetus hears inside the womb as blood pulses through
the placenta. I will never possess you. I just imagine holding you for a
moment, but really can you hold the water?

birches   **blues**

Birches are X-rays of hands. They swirl in myriad wakes like minnows.
Antlers comb our paths home. We began by evanescence. Its bark expands
in the light and sheds its speckled skin. Molecules of eyes cut deep the
snow until it bleeds blue. Bet Alef. *We would like only for once to get where
we are already.* A largest living organism. Stretching for acres and seas.
47,000 stems sprout from the root of one tree. This is a reproduction of.
Molecules bounce off and detour. Light scatters into blues. I wish they
took off like cranes, beating electric letters in the air. In a high wind the
leaves will clump together. The branches tangle and mesh into windows.
Until leaves turn into wings. The birches watch us with omniscient
eyes. I make it linger. Your eyes nest in me, so close that I cannot see
myself. Only dark *duende.* Does it entangle or connect? *If one can't see a
connection, one must assume a decision.* I feed the words and don't let them
fly off. Almond the words. Grain them. Eye the insides of their panther
skins. Count them up count what is bitter. Spin their threads. In clacking
chambers clinkering courtyards. In a darkroom place them. In a negative
carrier. Feed luminous and dark *duende.*

when   one   travels   one might

When one travels one might hit the words. Should one dwell, so someone else might rest? My father takes me on an organized trip to Romania. I find myself being nasty and hated. I find myself being a visionary. My father takes people on a mountain hike, but forgets where. I want to help him so much that I only keep praying. Prayer is really an attention. One day it becomes pregnant and through my mouth splits open. *Pietrleni Dominei.* A big moment yellow. The word, a bottomless pit. It is anima apex. Perhaps the Shadows of our Forgotten Ancestors. We detour from the road to a monastery. People fight. When one travels, one might heat the words. Monastery splits open. As we are in hot water, this is our last resort. Encounter, a linguistic cousin of country. A monk looks inside my eyes. I ask him to report all he sees. Beads of English trickle down his Mouth. The Icon was flying, he says. And Mother of God was there. Fragrant petals her tears. Her Face kept sowing. I prayed every night she would not appear to me. It is a cascade. I wish they took off like cranes. Her face keeps sowing. And the angers take off beating their electric letters in the air.

trees — x rays
   of hands

Your mother gave you a ginkgo leaf before she died: a thousand-year-old
inhabitant of the Permian oceans grows inside us. We understand well
cambium cells of waiting. We began with evanescence and now we think
of each other in terms of light. Do you see a mustard seed in a mulberry
tree? We would like only for once to get where we are already.
My mother, too, is an entrapped ghost, her venous mesh of neurons
colliding in cacophonies, her head full of yellow secrets. Their leaves push
me forward. I walk the Manhattan streets to meet her, I kneel and pick
more ginkgo leaves and wield them like oars. 51 cranes scraping the sky
with the geometry of crosses. Before I leave,
my mother stops in a park and collects—the groves inside us.

it   *was*   *4 pm*

My Mother used to collect cactuses. To see pink luscious fruit grow out
of them. *We would like only for once to get where we are already.* In storms,
I close the windows and open the doors. This is the size of my radiance.
Love is pinching. When threatened or amorous, the devilfish will bare the
brightly decorated inner surfaces of its pectoral fins, warning intruders
of its venomous spines. It took 10 million years to create the Grand
Canyon, and now, in this instance, it becomes mine. Explosion that occurs
simultaneously everywhere. It is a belonging that takes 2,000 years. One
must have been hurt and listless not to see a face. Amidst rocks. Native
Americans believed these were people whom a coyote-trickster changed
into boulders. Like monks they climb their faces up. Petrified prayers.
Inverted cathedrals. Hoodoos with anti-corrosive caps. Each gaze, a
prayer? Or: funny asparagus reminiscing. What are their true desires
in this disguise? It's not your face I desire. It is something inside. It
is not your body. Something inside where I cannot arrive. Instead the
topology of air bubbles. And always 3.59 pm. Just one minute away from
a true encounter. Trapped air inside a soap bubble—separated from other
trapped air by smoothly carved surfaces. How much would a soap bubble
cost, if there was only one in the world? Instead multiplicity of bubbled
faces. Can they inflate? The world is an egg.

to change your language

you must   change   your life

What's the evidence of belonging? The first day my mother takes me to the City Hall to issue my new ID. I am 162 cm tall. My eyes the color of beer. Granules spilled all over. Innumerable lids that lift open. I am at home and I write in English. If I could just cup this place in my hands. But place changes into a hedgehog and whirls into needles. The face of my city is that of an old volcano that spewed its interior & collapsed unto itself. Ithaca is a test of your nerves. Places are extensions of people. The largest living organism. Bodily here in relation to an already known there or set of there, where, here. This wakes demons. They swirl in myriad wakes like minnows. Alpine Tundra endured ice age only to break down under one single tread. When one travels, one might hit the words. What illness springs from a place that never was? Miniscule plots that explode hair and nails, growing straight into the belly of a frozen whale. In vain I wait for your eruptions. I see grebes building the nest there. What are the true desires in this disguise? It takes centuries for Arctic plants to spread over the surface of water.

unconscious   is   unconscious

Is repetition a repression? Do you see a mulberry tree in a mustard seed?
What illness springs from the lost place? Gulping the black milk of
mother tongue. If you scoop the place into your hands, it will disperse
into beads and venues. High-strung beads. Which dispersed. I'm trying
to collect them now. All cure is a voyage to the bottom of repetition.
Repetition changes nothing in the object repeated, but does change
something in the mind that contemplates it. Presents encroach one upon
another. There is a nobility in asking the same thing over and over. What
if this place is not a matter of arbitrary placing? Repetition is virginal.
Mnemosyne. Before we forget what we knew we have to recover what we
have forgotten. Underneath the large noisy events, lie the small events of
silence. *Ontikonos. If one can't see a connection, one must assume a decision.* She
thinks the moment she lets them in, she will settle for less and she will
have to book her flights there forever. Watch it grow—watch it contain
multitudes. Neurons are rising trees. What are the true desires in this
disguise? Metonymy is love disincarnate. Particled skin, feet, fingers.
Laughing kookaburras fly. His thing will not pick up the phone and make
music to her sustained existence. She wants to be an envelope stamped
with light.

today   *the taste*   *of*   *guava*

On a bus from Oxford to Cambridge a bus driver weeps. It is a loud
weeping. After a while a man approaches him and offers some help.
Things break in order to reveal. The bus driver says his grandmother
died. A big moment yellow. Only after the funeral, at the cemetery, my
face resurrected. With a serenity. I saw her in a white wedding dress
with my grandfather. The man kneels and prays for her. The bus driver
stops weeping. We are riding. We are on the road. And I get to where I
want. Little blobs of colors. Little blobs of juice. What a wedding feast.
And a star-fruit. Burnham Ovary. How to express the sound the masts of
boats make? The whole village of masts chatting, clacking, clinkering.
The congregation of lepers with bells? And did you know that sand is a
cemetery and souls whirl and seep into your multiples? Did you know
that sand is a foggy land? *Kraina na bosaka.* We strand everything by a
metaphor. One can say: the reeds rustle. Or: the reeds are enamored by
wind. They swing and sway. They bow. They tend into the sea.
This is the music of their longing. Yet they swing back into their vertical
position and distraught amidst all their restlessness they root.

On the train from Vien to Lublana an American from CO tells me I have
a beautiful smile. I get off and I say "Chwała." We meet in Be Café. He
has an olive shirt and a green bike. Something about him that lingers.
Where I cannot get. In Pirano the masts of the boats go silent. The house
stench. It is in contrast to yesterday's liveliness. Just when I reprimand
myself for smiling too much an American girl approaches me in the
restroom and says: you have a beautiful smile. You sing of me America. I
am very short but your dream song makes me grow 10 centimeters a day.
This is unstoppable. A measure of your love. A barometer. When I am a
giant will you still love me? Wherever a word goes, it puts up a tent. It
is strange we meet again. Perhaps you should not catch a joy as it flies.
Almond the words. In negative carrier place them. In clacking chambers
clinkering courtyards. Water them bathe them cleanse them. Shush them.
Cradle them. Invoke their ghosts. Under light sensitive case. Put them on
a linen. Hang them. Line them with cloth pins. Pray to them. Embark.

Children swing on a rope down to a river. Water is shocked by this splutter. We stay on shore, even though we know the water is master of gravitation and will save us from flight. Unlike Mary's Yes, a swing into hearts ajar.

I dream of the day when my syllables will hold rough wood, my letters will be sewn in a stove or fireplace. It's not the sacrifice we resist, but the beauty. The intensity of the instance burns. For it has to turn into another instance. There is nobility in asking the same thing over and over.

Children swing on a rope down to a river. Water is shocked by this splutter. The truth burns us before it falls away. We remain on shore.

When did she start to witness evanescence? The animals saw her suffering in light and saw that it was good and took her light in suffering. A cat died after she left. Life was not enough. The occasional splutter of light. The simplicity of smile. There is nobility in asking.

Children swing on a rope down to a river.

Nico's Aya speaks of light and evanescence. The blessing of his Grandmother. Woven DNA patterns. Now it has holes and no warmth, but the child holds onto it and repeats: "AYA's church." Not knowing that Aya, his grandmother, wove him into Being.

There were many blankets. The plants saw and knew it was good. There is nobility in weaving the same blanket over and over. We are impatient to rid ourselves of time. It takes centuries for Arctic plants to spread and form a quaking mat, a circumference of clarities.

annunciation　　*of*　　　　　　　　　*cells*

this　rain　is　a　bouquet　of　cells　she

brought　him　yesterday　magnified　under　their　eyes

into　honeycombs

Between　climbing ferns　and　pergolas—rock exposures

Kudzu　lapis lazuli

A　pensive　choir　of　tanzanite　owls

(Or are these oleanders?).

The　silent　touch　on　her　arm –

a　ginkgo　tree　grows　there

and　leaves　her with　white

Nucleus

Like these raindrops like this waltz like a delicate netting in

them and　something　in　her　understands　these　cells are

celestial

and　they　become the silver　foxes

of rain　her　inner　tears　skyscrapers

and chromosomes get entangled and make music

ERA IV

homing   *instincts*

Ornithologists say white-feathered pigeons are masters of survival.
While I was giving a reading in Chicago, Jan 28th at 5 pm, the roof of
the pigeon exhibit in Chorzów, Poland collapsed under the weight of
snow. 63 people died. Słowo nie zagruchotało. To tylko dach gruchnął. An
iridescent audience on air. Archangels Barbs Homers Frillbacks Laughers
Modenas Nuns Orliks. Swarming to the last of the roof. Dodging what is
falling. Waiting for their owners in dead silence. While I invoke syllables,
give offerings in Chicago. How unexpectedly something will rustle just
a morpheme away. Poetry is a maker of white and the heaviness of white
makes the roofs collapse. Brodawczaki. Garłacze. Latawce. Turkoty.
Perukarze. Mewki. Pawiki. Błyskotki szafirowe. Poezja zawsze siè spóznia
jak paryska dziewczyna na obcasach. Przylatuje na miejsce tragedii *post
factum*. Poetry comes late like a Parisian girl in high heels at the scene
of the tragedy *post factum*. Poetry, a prayer which saves only itself. Poetry
arrives late. A pigeon that did not get back to the Arc but waves its olive
branch from afar. And takes off on extended letters.

pentecost 3

Are you living underground? Have you split a peyote button and are practicing Tango Milonga on your cross-country skis with some newly found hot ski-bums? Are you off to Colorado to betray me with some children and Peter Pans? Have you jumped off a ski lift? Are you angry with your past? Does your skin break out in boils? Do strangers make odd faces at you—expressive of infinite remorse? Do phantom string quartets play mute rhapsodies in your left ear? Is your right ear occupied by the voice of a little man saying over and over "joy to our students"? Is your morning cereal soggier than in the past? Do you think your car is holding a grudge for some unexplained grievance in the past? Is your heater on constantly though the room remains cold? Has God appeared to you saying, "It was only a joke"? If one or all of these symptoms is present, I can well understand the eerie silence coming from the northern lands where you now reside. Here, all is the sunlight of the twilight days of the new warmer globe. Soon vast jungles of rubber and teak trees will take over the potato fields and snakes and jaguars will frolic on our front lawn. Since you are closed in the ZOO, you sigh and say, "I'm home."

to   a   universe   of

seahorse

Unkempt philosopher of silence with a dermal cirri. *Baron rampante.*
Drumming vespers to an audience of bleached coral. Your zebra stripes
transplanted into medicinal plates. I bought myself a sextant to measure
the angle of your elevation, so I can always see where the current takes
you. One should not catch a joy as it floats. A snout hopper
of the ineffable. Little prince, how I would like to fetch you a juicy
shrimp. For heart is a secret seahorse. Choreographer of chromatophores.
I see underwater hourglasses waving through a spiral of rings. Coralline
algae. Orange sponge. Aria of anemones and gorgonians. Abducted
from your bed of emerald eelgrass and anapest of hued pigment. What
illness springs from a lost place? I am just on the other side of the mirror.
Lexicons trespass; there are cross-code breakdowns. I am seized by your
vertigo flapping of knobs and spines. A hermit with no stomach. Epicure
of jaffa cake. A beige enclosure. Built of Atoms & Light. We began with
evanescence.

dear hoopoe,

I was away having *a bongo bliss* on the snowy slopes; watching the white albatrosses fall from the sky; contemplating the nature of snow dunes and the waltz of water flowers. I had a dream of Chinese Circus, Ricotta Pie, and Columbus Manatee Mermaid. I was exploring the land of Genghis Khan—the most ruthlessly violent, mercilessly cunning monsters united by drinking blood from their horses' necks. I was contemplating the "burning bushes," "doves," "manna," and other signs of divine madness. I was following the dreams of Tanzanite owls. I walked on the frozen lake and spilled all syllables; now their vowels and consonants paddle inside the white grains of hourglasses. Now the purgatory souls of poems inhabit me and ask for word-relations. Forgive me this self-inflicted exile and unknown presence rapping on your door with draughts of light.

dear marauder

What a beautiful Yinguo owl nests on Ginkgo Biloba trees perched
briskly in my mailbox! Who could lacerate it? Not even a fierce editor
like me! After all, editors are human species who show themselves to be
human, as Higginson once wrote in *Atlantic Monthly*. It is well enough
to remember this fact, when you approach Me. I am *not a gloomy despot, no
Nemesis or Rhadamanthus (...) draw near me, therefore, with soft approaches &
mild persuasions*. Meanwhile, on a more personal note, I'm terribly jealous
because I know that the fact I haven't heard from you in months means
you have no need for my odd impossible companionship because you have
two or three new boys. Either that or you fought a duel with Kasia and
lost. Sorry if that's the case.
Please let me know where to send flowers.
P.S. 1. I had a sexy dream about you today. In this dream you were not
even afraid of me.
P.S. 2. I don't know what else to say! Perhaps I would gain the respect I've
long deserved and your timely response, if I were to publish a short essay
in Playboy. Yes, Playboy. Snort at my dreams if you like, but if I did get
published there, I might receive an invitation to the mansion. I would be
sitting with bunnies while you shivered in New England snow.
P.S. 3. Plus, the Playboy credentials would make me very expensive as a
campus visitor. It would make me quite chic. How would you like that?

first   time

The first manifestation of being a poet was when my jeans got stuck in the chain of a bicycle. I was pedaling home, my jeans swaying to the staccato rhythm. When they got in, the world halted. My pants, sucked in by the great wheel of the universe and before them their life flashed which is to say the whole of my wardrobe. My left leg was desperately thrashing and flapping, but the right one was not meeting it, if it went on, my left knee would be destroyed. For a moment dangling uselessly back and forth. The only way to detach myself was to desert the bicycle and pants caught red-handed in a mortal embrace with a machine which according to Chinese people, *is a little mule, led along by its ears & spurred on with a shower of foot blows*. I have to slow down this moment to take off my pants and run through the street to my door in my red panties. The finish line was filled with determination, twists and turns of the key at the wooden door like a neurotic woodpecker.

I want you to know a big battle happened here. Kind of a *Tour de France*. I contemplated grafting a little commemorative plate at the exact place of the event. Now I do it over and over again, stripping myself more voluntarily yet still pretending it's an accident. Discovering the secret pleasures of syntactical spokes, syllabic nakedness.

pentecost 4

I think you've lost my mind. Either that or I have to write about it
till it makes some sort of poetic sense. I just had a dream about being
dismembered. You woke me up from that dream. Didn't you call me
modern Orpheus the other day? *If we go down into ourselves we find that we
possess exactly what we desire.* Or take Lorca's ant, who climbed a tree to
see the eyes we carry inside us. The ant gave her life for those eyes. The
beauty of our friendship is helping each other love what we love. *Distance
is the Soul of Beauty.* It was a song that killed Orpheus. The twigs and other
missiles did not get him. Ciconian Maenads used their own hands only in
order to share. Even while floating down the river, he continued singing!
And sycamores and stalactites swayed in unison. I wish they would take
off on extended letters. Quarrels ceased. Mermaids or manatee ceased to
dismember wandering sailors. Orpheus with the sounds of his lyre created
a forest, a chorus of trees. His voice transgressed existence.

pa　　*ra*　　*dos*

They are built like oven birds, the poets. Not the larks, nightingales, Tanzanite owls, modenas, orliks, but these small migratory birds whose repetitive song consists of: *a poem a poem a poem.* Tough little lives of ovenbirds. Half of all adults die. Half of Polish poets die, of self-inflicted exiles, excessive vodka, envy, a tiger or heavy labor. Some of them die struck by an orange—an unusual epiphany.

Ovenbirds die young and lonely. They leave layers of riddles, odes, villanelles and a song goes on dismembered. Ovenbirds do not overlap their songs. It is song that kills ovenbirds. A tedious poem. Not the trills and jitters. A sexless song—wrenched out of want. Necessary birds, ovenbirds clench their wings and ask: Lord-bird "why did you make me an oven bird"?

Ovenbirds are so modest and small they surrender to their part of the song. They never see their work as a whole (not even with a jar of fireflies in their homes). Their voices transgress the whole forests and take off on extended morphemes. They pause, and then sing one after the other again, for up to 40 songs.

raw reds

My mom gives me yet another map. She marks a new road with erasable pencil. I learn avenues: Wolf, Alvernic, Newkirk. She is a cartographer who sneaked out of previous maps—too real—in search of a telescoped phantom map frayed with scraps of water. What are the true desires in this disguise? She twitches, wiggles, and grabs for new territories, pennies on the road. With her eyes, she makes the holes in the map. Each side of our hemisphere sees the opposite half, such is chiasm. I fold and unfold the map learning it like a new sense, line by line. I trace the qualia with my fingers; the effervescent needles to the air. I listen for the foghorns of relay stations. The persistence of synapses. Look, these pearls were once. We follow the hummingbirds' routes, the number of elementary doors. *We would like for once to get where we are already.* With the recharge rates of hearts beating on their wings; the probing needles of air-conquistadors. The phantom maps live in vagaries of my mom's *magna carta*.

evidence   *yellow*   *grains*

Whenever we visited, my grandfather would put his chair on the road
and wait. *Kraina na Bosaka*. We were the apparition of deer. Pray, why
chase each stalk of wounded light? Awaiting us on a dusty road memory,
inseparable from desire. Just like yesterday: we opened the door for the
arrival of Elijah and then closed it again. *We would like for once to get where
we are.* Only children can find *afikoman*. We remain on shore.
We wait on a dusty road. While fasting on bitter herb—*maror*. We wait
for *Belshazzar* scribbled on the wall. We walk on a frozen lake and spill
the syllables into dusk. The purgatory souls inhabit us. We are their
morphemes. The windows wait under a black chador. I wish the chairs
would grow wings. For a new syllable contains all morphemes, faces,
gestures, and every other syllable in no man's land so dwindled, little,
in the end it weighs.

in   va   sion

Today I keep   undressing   the   trees

ring   by   ring   where I cannot

reach until   intimate   vulnerable they stretched

into coiling snakes,

and I keep stripping the bark to its cambium cells

to the tap roots.

Ancient migrants with accreted brackets.

Some travelers sit on their luggage long before departure.

The woods cool off the fire that consumes us. You gave me

a backpack full of bees to guide me so you could see where

the paths took me.

I hold the touch, the bark, until cortex trans

forms   into *kora* in my native lungs, but also a maiden

examining forget-me-nots, carried into an underworld of roots.

An abduction, an ancient wedding ritual,

her mother mad from grief, her father shrinking into beehives.

CODA

arrivals

An uncle from America paid us a visit. He was dressed in a tight blue
container. Of a metallic flavor. It was the first time we'd seen him
buttoned up. And the sight gripped us. Right by our throats. Only
his blue water lily drifted, unbuttoned, maybe somewhere else and not
on time. Dropping in unexpectedly in the night, he would steal to the
cupboard to munch our onions. What are the true desires in this disguise?
He settled among the plots of wreaths. *We would like only for once to get
where we are already.* Maybe an unknown instrument in its case. Later the
men from the special brigade tossed him. Like a birthday boy. It seemed

as if he'd fallen   from   the sky   straight

onto a trampoline   bounced   off

and   then,

he was irretrievably   lost

Is it my imagination or my dad grows an inch every second week?
This growth seems to be unstoppable. He will age into a giant. Ovid
would testify to dads becoming baobabs and that's what I fear. To kiss
his cheeks, we will have to climb a tree whose wrinkled bark grows
omniscient eyes. Now the branches where he used to perch will perch
on him and comb his hair. One would expect from their dad a rather
slow shrinking; their gracious dwindling or slow disappearance into an
ant or almond. No, our dad grows antlers and every now and then sheds
them in clacking clinkering chambers. He grafts his presence on all the
tables. Piles of papers stacked in every room. Dust accompanies my dad
to the higher ranks of heaven. At first he used to mark small territories
with little envelopes; opened and unopened business letters; blackened
combs of honey. (For bees he was rather a large looking cosmonaut with
his out of blue accordion or giant brass hoopoe with a satchel.) In one
room he spreads mountains of emblems and badges of merit. Nonchalant
medals. He used to carry people over the mountains. Now he could carry
mountains over the people. Wherever his word enters, it puts up a tent.
In another room, a garden of receipts like sleeping white ptarmigans
that will suddenly lift off and swirl in trills and jitters when the door
and window synchronize their yawning. These plots of insurrections will
rise and sell the house with its little coupons. Due to these growths, we
quietly empty the house. My younger sister, however, testifies that dad
grows proportionally to the very size of our evacuation. I don't dare to use
a big word: but I will say it: "There are moments I see him waving to me
from some transcontinental space."

hagio graphia

My mother transforming into a martyr. First she read the stories of
saints, especially Saint Jadwiga, the queen of Poland. Next symptom: her
proclamation of death caused by my refusal to cooperate, for example,
to eat ham. Another step towards sainthood. She asked her neighbors
and relatives to testify in writing to her goodness and sanity. She asked
for examples. She handed me all the letters at the airport. I keep them
unopened and believe in aspen leaves' trembling. They air the air.

I was afraid to touch the brush she used, lest it become a relic. I also
stopped flushing the toilet. The important thing is that she herself is a
relic—some even testified to seeing her spread like a cross. She displayed
the signs of bilocation. Small displacements. First she displaced her pain
onto my sleeves, then onto the geographies. We would see her preaching
to congregations of jays in California and she flickered in a drunken
woman sitting on a railway station in Kursk. She was in New York
chatting with a Bulgarian guitarist. Not to mention her Tartar cheeks,
which were ubiquitous and gave rise to little halos. Once she saw me and
told me her yellow secret and we spent the rest of the afternoon collecting
ginkgo leaves shaped like the Permian oceans.

{....}

Every day she is parting from them. She is burying her parents in staccato rhythm trembling like aspen leaves little farewells restlessness that will not allow hurting itself. It's a hovering burial like a hummingbird which calculates the recharge rates to extract its nectar. Is it selfish to prepare yourself like that? To construct more than one funeral? Isn't one flower really 30 flowers? Junipers are silver moons. The growth on the trees are tricks of light, the dead winking. Every parting is accompanied by verbal abuse. They say the nastiest things just to make the goodbye easier. Sun hits as many needles as possible. She buries them every day. Diseased trees gnarl their hands looking for invisible hooks.

the roads   diverged   in   a   wood
and   I   took   all   of   them

There are places where all unspeakables nestle
      What's unuttered   flutters

unborn   designs   circle   over   unpatched
roofs

non-arrivals and never-endings   dart

                  up   from   unfettered

bliss   orphaned chances   take on unabated

meaning
                  sprouts swarm in

         numbers only
                  forget-me-nots would know

                  there   are   places

na   no   la

They thistle in us. They speck in the morning. They tingle. Sorrelic
apparitions. There is a tigress mother wanting to trim your hair. They
come to us. Do you hear them? Some as heavy footsteps. Others—
miniscule kisses. Thin as grass. Rising and swaying parasols. They come
with swinging hips. They come as minnows. They try to get where they
belong. They come in wrinkles. They come as a host of molecules. They
come as hard-faced dybbuks. They swarm into this lighthouse. They
have fancy hats. With forget-me-nots. They pebble across the floor. They
fall from marigold trees and lie crucified on the road. Get up and sing.
They pinch like too much love. They trespass. They arrive at a wailing
wall. They dot. We are burying them every day. We are burying them in
staccato rhythm. They rise and accrete. They beat electric letters in the air.
They hop always to a higher branch. They come invincible. They come
to torture. They come to soothe. They come for romance. They flip and
tremble tiny farewells. They come as mustards seeds. Do you see them in a
mulberry tree? They slide down the needles. They come as growth on wolf
trees, the dead winking. They air the air. They come to forgive. They ask
for forgiveness. They come as hyphae. They come as hostages. They come
as clogged streets. They come in slow trains. They come as silver jaguars.
Burning bushes, doves, manna, the blood of horses' necks. They come as
purgatory souls. They chip off the wall. In loops and whorls. They want
to rent one line. They want to breakdown. They re-colonize. They come
to insulate us with snow. They come in giggles. They come in almonds.
They come to eye us, inside our panther skins. We bury them. They
come in black chadors. They rap on our door with churned up grains,
tides, whispers. They come as drafts of juniper. They spread on the floor
as a cross. They are relics of grief and light. They perch on branches like
monk hedgehogs. They come as juncos. They come in lekking crowds.
They come in high-strung beads and scatter into our vessels. They
come in volcanic lavish. They come as noble Odysseuses. They hover as
hummingbirds, calculating their rates of return. We bury them. They air
the air. They are ubiquitous as Tartar cheeks. They bilocate. They come as
yellow secrets.

NOTES

Title "Strata" signifies in my native language "a loss."

Era I

what's the evidence
Kraina na bosaka—from Polish: the land that runs barefoot.

Encounter is a linguistic cousin of country—from Edward Casey's *Getting Back Into Place*.

I lose home every time
Some of the thoughts in this piece have been inspired by Heidegger's "Building Dwelling Thinking;" Edward Casey's *Getting Back into Place*; and some of Gertrude Stein's ideas.

Encounter is a linguistic cousin of country
We would like only for once to get where we are already—quotes from Edward Casey's *Getting Back into Place*.

is there something down   by the water keeping itself from
us?
Above tagline is from Mark Strand's opening line of the poem "Our Masterpiece Is the Private Life." Some of the thoughts were inspired by reading Jorie Graham (Never "Prayer") and Ammons, as well as Dante's Divine Comedy.

today light in itself
If you could only grasp that you are not the center of things. The center is He, and He, too, finds no love—a quote from Karol Wojtyła's poem: "To A Girl Disappointed in Love."

Era II

topology   must   triumph

A fish in water that suffers of thirst. A sponge suffering, because it cannot saturate itself. A river, suffering because the reflections of clouds and trees are not clouds and trees – a quote from Miłosz's prose poem: "Esse."

death most reveals itself by single shoes
There is no there, there
Gertrude Stein in *Everybody's Autobiography* (1937), a remark concerning the fact that her childhood home in California no longer existed.

the roads
the idea of possible universes has been inspired by reading physics (especially Hawkins).
the idea of multiple polarity of text has been inspired by Eco's *The Role of the Reader.*
the idea of holding the water has been inspired by Anne Carson's poems.

snow a martyr
first three lines are after Robert Creeley's poem: "The Business."

pentecost I
If we go down into ourselves we find that we possess exactly what we desire—
Simone Weil's line.

would fire be so gentle
The motion of "now" occurs in a time shorter than the blink of an eye, since a second of time delineates a segment of space spread out like a 186,000-mile-long caterpillar. Imagine you are Alice, as you move through this "caterpillar" at ever-increasing speed—a quote from Leonard Shlain's book, *Art and Physics. Can you hold the water?*—a quote from Anne Carson's poem.

Era III

each day   *a crescendo*
some of ideas have been inspired by Heidegger and Edward Casey.

birches blues
If one can't see a connection, one must assume a decision—a quote from Hejinian.

when one travels one might
The tagline is a reference to Hejinian's My Life.
The word, a bottomless pit—an appropriation of a quote from Hejinian's *My Life.*

Era IV

Dear Hoopoe,
bongo bliss—a line from Tim Horvath's short story: "The Eighth Hour."

Ewa Chrusciel is a bilingual poet and a translator. She has two other books of poems in English (besides this reprint of *Strata*): they are *Contraband of Hoopoe* published by Omnidawn in 2014 & *Of Annunciations* published by Omnidawn in 2017. She also writes in Polish and published three books of poems in Poland. She translated Jack London, Joseph Conrad, I.B. Singer as well as Jorie Graham, Kazim Ali, Lyn Hejinian, Cole Swensen and other American poets into Polish. She is an Associate Professor of Humanities at Colby-Sawyer College.

Strata
by Ewa Chrusciel

Cover painting by Julie Püttgen: *Cloudmapping: Becalmed*, 2008.
Watercolor and gouache on paper, 16"x12"
www.108namesofnow.com & www.unlessanduntil.info.

Cover typeface: Kabel LT Std
Interior typefaces: Garamond 3 LT Std

Cover & interior design by Cassandra Smith

Offset printed in the United States
by Edwards Brothers Malloy, Ann Arbor, Michigan
On 55# Glatfelter B18 Antique
Acid Free Archival Quality Recycled Paper

Publication of this book was made possible in part by gifts from:
The New Place Fund
The Clorox Company Foundation

Omnidawn Publishing
Oakland, California
2018
Rusty Morrison & Ken Keegan, senior editors & co-publishers
Trisha Peck, managing editor & program director
Gillian Olivia Blythe Hamel, senior poetry editor
Cassandra Smith, poetry editor & book designer
Sharon Zetter, poetry editor, book designer & development officer
Liza Flum, poetry editor
Avren Keating, poetry editor & fiction editor
Juliana Paslay, fiction editor
Gail Aronson, fiction editor
Tinia Montford, marketing assistant
Emily Alexander, marketing assistant
Terry A. Taplin, marketing assistant
Matthew Bowie, marketing assistant
SD Sumner, copyeditor